E-Banking: Namibia's SMB Growth Engine

E-Banking: Namibia's SMB Growth Engine

Daniel Almeida

Friends forever, come what may

TABLE OF CONTENTS

Chapter 1

Introduction

1.1   Research background

The evolution and development of technology has transformed many spheres of life in Namibia. This include the change in traditional aspects ranging from the way banking was conducted in the past to the modern technological banking. This change in banking development has brought different risks and values in the banking sector which was not experienced in the past. "Electronic banking is described by (Nouri,1387) as the availability of banking services to customers by secure media and without physical presentations, while mobile banking defined as ''the payment for goods and services made between two parties through a mobile device'' (Jacob, 2007).

In Namibia, this development in the uses of electronic banking is not matured yet, such as not yet utilized by small and medium customers although the sufficient enabling infrastructures are in place. These segments of customers are still using lots of cash and transfer in the branches to effect payments to other parties whilst ignoring the modern and convenient way of banking. Small and medium businesses are recognized as the sources and drives of the economic growth and sustainability, and to create robust opportunities of employment.

Namibia is one of the countries that has high unemployment rate and the government has recently created platforms supported by injection of funds to vigorously boost these business operators to assist in socio economic upliftment.

The uses of electronic banking will not only reduce the high cost associated with the traditional banking, it also reduces the high burden of cost incurred by the bank in the form of overtime salary payment and efficiency in the bank process. The diversification into banking process is intended to shift the banking paradigm from the high cost to efficient, convenient and cheap banking system to pre-empt losing the clients to newly opened mobile payment operators.

1.2   Problem statement

The banks in Namibia are always full of customers who are mainly drawing, deposit, and transferring payments to suppliers, third parties and are overloading employees. The overloading of attending to clients doing basic banking such as transfers and withdrawing are contributing to employees working overtime and placing additional cost to the bank in terms of overtime payment and logistic supports. The objective to introduction of internet and mobile banking technologies was to create another channel of banking which allows clients to execute banking activities at their places which allow banks to save on logistic costs (FNB Namibia, 2011). It is well known that corporate clients have adopted the use of electronic banking contrary to the SME clients hence this banking channel is not practically working for the SME clients although complimented with client benefits in terms of convenience, time and cost savings due to short in lack of data. This paper seek to identify and clarify the barriers that are hindering the adoption of electronic (internet and mobile) usage by businesses in Namibia and highlights the benefits associated with uses of electronic banking by small and medium enterprises (SME) in order to embrace the digital opportunities and risks presented by the imminent fourth industrial revolution in managing their business life (Deloitte Insight, 2018). It will also provide recommendations to SMEs regarding their contribution to the Namibian economy in the context of electronic banking. Electronic banking especially mobile is very popular in east Africa (Africa Business Communities 2018), hence our approach will consider pre-emptive strategy of not losing our client to internet network provider in this context.

What are the principal factors the adoption of electronic banking by the small medium enterprises? The specific questions include;

- What factors influences SMEs intention to adopt the internet banking?

- What factors influences SMEs intention to adopt the mobile banking?

- What factors determines SMEs usage of internet banking?

- What factors determines SMEs usage of mobile banking?

- How the intention to adopt the internet banking lead to usage of internet banking?

- How the intention to adopt the mobile banking lead to usage of mobile banking?

1.3   Objective of the study

The study will seek to argue on the benefits internet banking has brought to the business sector in general and to the small and medium enterprises in specific. The study seeks to examine the factors that influence the adoption of electronic banking by the small medium enterprises in Namibia. The specific objectives include;

- To examine the factors that influences SMEs intention to adopt the internet banking in Namibia.

- To examine the factors that influences SMEs intention to adopt the mobile banking in Namibia

- To examine the factors that influences SMEs usage of internet banking in Namibia

- To examine the factors that influences usage of mobile banking in Namibia

- To examine the effect of intention to adopt the internet banking on usage of internet banking usage among SMEs in Namibia

- To examine the effect of SMEs intention to adopt the mobile banking on mobile banking usage among SMEs in Namibia

1.4   Theoretical relevance of the study

The usage of electronic banking which encompass both mobile and internet is on the increase in some developing country more importantly South Africa where volumes of payments are made for business sourcing and used to conduct financial services (Institute of Bankers, 2018). Studies have been carried out to find the barriers impacting the adoption of internet and mobile payments, collections and their benefits. However there is no study done in Namibia so far. Therefore, this study is an attempt at reflecting the factors affecting the adoption and usage of internet and mobile payments technologies by small and medium businesses in Namibia and whether the usage will enhance and improve their operations.

1.5   Practical relevance and beneficiary

The study will benefit the small and medium businesses in cost savings and streamlining of their business processes as well as general business operators who are not using electronic payment methods outside Windhoek. The commercial banking sector in streamlining their service delivery channels, saving on costs of paying employees and country wide expansion of branches, the internet and mobile service provider to expand the revenue base, the government in terms of regulation and ensure all citizen have access to banking.

1.6   Societal relevance

The benefits of this research will formulate methods and understanding to SME to fully adopt the usage of the banking technology to improve their processes and include large number of clients which increases the creation of employments in Namibian society. It will also contribute to the existence of literatures and models that are relevant to improvement of standard of living in the wider society.

1.7   Personal interest

The study is central to the researcher as he is in charge of the SME funding and business improvement at the Development Bank of Namibia (DBN). The topic is very interesting in the researcher's career development and sustainability of the bank in the future. The research helps to fill the linkages in literature and provide insights on benefits from the adoption of internet and mobile banking. The study is also vital to the beneficiaries to acquire knowledge and develop relevant strategies that create positive synergies on economy from utilization of electronic banking technologies.

1.8   Application of concepts

Performance expectancy stresses the degree the SME' clients believe that internet and mobile banking technology will have a substantial benefit to their businesses; effort expectancy introduce the degree of easiness associated with the use of the internet and banking technology; Social influence stresses the judgments the SMEs receive from peers and society by using electronic banking system, while facilitating conditions stresses the importance of sufficient infrastructural support to enable the client to make use of the electronic banking. The use of the electronic banking is further moderated by the price value of facilitating resources, hedonic motivation present the joy and novelty seeking in the uses of technology while habit of clients on the technology use moderate the experience effect on electronic banking.

The Unified Theory of Acceptance and Use of Technology (UTAUT) will guide the researcher to predict the SMEs behavioral intention on the uses of electronic banking. The model guide the study to formulate the electronic banking technology as a dependent variable on the factor determinants of performance expectancy, effort expectancy, social influence, hedonic motivation, Price value, habit, behavioral intention and facilitating conditions as independent variables. The researcher will use binary logistic regression models to predict the relationship between independent and dependent variables. Regression analysis is commonly used for prediction and forecasting, and determination of how the dependent variable changes due to the change in independent variables. (Groebner, D.F. et al. 2008).

1.9   Assumption and delimitation of the scope of study

The research is conducted outside Windhoek, Namibia and will be limited to small and medium enterprises customers only, specifically the semi-formal traders such as small garage owners, brick making projects, shebeen owners, small events coordinators such traditional weddings and funerals, events tents hire and meat traders. The researcher has interviewed one head of retail banking of commercial bank and a marketing manager of mobile payment company in Namibia for their future strategy in the mobile transfer market. It will focus on clients that are banking with commercial banks and assumed to be a sample that represent the whole population of small and medium enterprises in the whole country. The study will not focus on the entire design of the bank' electronic banking, it will only concentrate on the payment, collections and transfers, however it is to some extent constrained by the following factors: time, finance and dearth of information.

1.10   Organization of Research

The research is divided into the following 5 chapters:

• Chapter 1 is the introduction where there is a background of the study, statement of the problem, objectives of the study, research questions and finally the organization of the research. Chapter 2 is literature review, whereby the researcher reviews the related theoretical literature and concepts of the study; Methodology will be presented in Chapter 3, Chapter 4 deals with the research findings and discussion, while the conclusion and recommendations of the study are presented in Chapter 5.

Chapter 2

Literature Review and Theoretical Framework

2.1   Introduction

This chapter focuses on literature review and other empirical studies done by previous researchers in this field. It illustrates the historical development of internet and mobile banking and the subsequent developmental trends up to current usage globally and Namibia, in particular.

2.2   Theoretical framework: Unified Theory of Acceptance and the Use of Technology (UTAUT2)

UTAUT2 is a basic technological model developed as a comprehensive synthesis of prior technology and it is extended from the basic UTAUT model (Venkatesh et al, 2003). The model has four original constructs, independent variables that are performance expectancy, effort expectancy, social influence and facilitating condition that influence the behavioural intention. UTAUT2 extend from the extrinsic behavioural intention to use to three intrinsic motivation constructs and independent variables which are hedonic motivation, price value and habit. The UTAUT2 constructs are discussed in this section.

2.2.1   Performance Expectancy (PE)

Performance expectancy is the extent to which the usage of internet and mobile technology product can provide the SMEs the benefits in performing their business activities. According to Venkatesh at el (2012), Performance expectancy is most important determinant in the banking technology adoption due to its perceived usefulness which the SMEs believe using a new technology can improve their job performance, the extrinsic motivation create perceptions among the SMEs that the new banking technology would perform an activity when such an activity is perceived to be instrumental in achieving valued outcomes that are different from the activity itself. Performance expectancy inform the SMEs on how the banking technology increases the business capabilities and relative cost advantage that the business gains in adopting the new banking technology.

2.2.2 Effort Expectancy (EE)

Effort expectancy refers to the degree which the SMEs perceive the ease of use associated with the usage of internet and mobile banking technology. Similar to performance expectancy in the internet and mobile banking technology adoption context, the effort expectancy is the most important determinants for analysing the mobile and internet banking technology usage behavior and the behavioral intention (Davis, 1989). According to Venkatesh at el, (2003). The effort expectancy influence how the SMEs perceived ease of use, free of effort or relative difficult to use and understand the banking technology, while the complexity of the banking technology can influence the SMEs attitude of use in both mandatory and voluntary usage.

2.2.3 Social Influences (SI)

The degree which the SMEs judge whether the social settings she/he lives influences the uses of internet and mobile banking technology. Under social influence the SME's behaviour think that they should use mobile and internet banking technologies because people who are important to them think that they should use mobile and internet technologies for learning. The people in the same setting are also supportive of the use of e-banking technologies.

2.2.4 Facilitating condition (FC),

The degree which the SMEs believe that organisational and technical infrastructure exist to support the uses of internet and mobile banking and other technologies. In this context, facilitating condition is the extent to which the SMEs believe that technical infrastructure exists to enhance the use of electronic banking. Facilitating conditions improve business efficiency and development of ideas by introducing a new paradigm which has strong implication on the use of the system. It represents the logistics and technical aids needed to use electronic banking by the SMEs.

2.2.5 Hedonic motivation (HM),

Hedonic motivation is defined as the fun or pleasure derived from using mobile or internet banking technology, and it has been shown to play an important role in determining technology acceptance and use (Brown and Venkatesh 2005). In this study, it is believed that hedonic motivation conceptualized as perceived enjoyment has been found to influence technology acceptance by the SMEs.

2.2.6 Perceived/Price value (PV),

The degree which the SMEs judge the cost of using the internet and mobile banking relative to the value and benefits they receive. Price value is defined as consumers' cognitive trade-off between the perceived benefits of the applications and the monetary cost for using them (Dodds et al. 1991). The price value is positive when the benefits of using the internet and mobile technology are perceived to be greater than the monetary cost and such price value has a positive impact on intention. Thus, price value is a predictor of the SMEs behavioral intention to use the banking technology.

2.2.7 Habit (HT),

The degree the SMEs think that the uses of internet and mobile banking technology has become part of their normal life and it is something that is associated with them when they think of banking activities. Habit is the extent to which the SMEs tend to perform behaviours automatically because of learning (Limayem et al. 2007), while Kim et al. (2005) equate habit with automaticity.

2.2.8 Behavioural Intention (BI),

Behavioural intention when SMEs think of taking an action. It is the direct independent variable for the use of technology in the UTAUT2 model. Behavioral intention is the degree to which the SME has formulated conscious plans to adopt or not adopt electronic banking in the future. It is predicted that actual adoption of electronic banking technology is always difficult hence behavioral intention is measured as the conative loyalty (Giovanis et al, 2013), which is an important goal in the adoption of electronic banking.

2.3 Electronic banking

Electronic payment is part of the electronic commerce which offers customers to make their payments to sell and buy goods or services over the internet channel of banking (American Education – E-Payment Definition 2008). Electronic banking offers value to customers 24 hours without having physical presence in the bank. It is the fastest growing mode of banking among the businesses and elite individuals worldwide. According to American Education, the uses of checks has declined from 85% of non –cash payments in 1979 to 59% in 2002. This is commonly due to the electronic banking taking centre stage in the development of technology to harness their operations

Electronic banking channels of banking system includes the uses of mobile and internet payments, credit cards, e-cash, e-cheques and stored value cards, however the most popular mode of payments are done through credit cards (Georgescu and Georgescu 2006). Many banks are refocusing their concentration of conducting their banking operations in an electronic manner which is more extensive and efficient than the traditional way of banking.

2.4 Concept of internet banking

Internet banking or online banking is a subset of electronic banking which include inte alia electronic financing. It is a new channel of banking that enables the buyers to effect payment over the internet and allows settlement with the sellers. The service enable businesses to transmit and payments and remittance data electronically over the internet with authentication, encryption and acknowledgement features (E-Business Technology Forecast, 2002). The mode of banking payment is conducted without a physical presence in the bank by making use of the computer (PC) or mobile phone connected to the web of the bank at their own location. Client requires a password that allows the accessibility to the bank's network on which the user's account is linked. The password represent the security code by which the account is connected and allow the client to access the account and effect the transfer of money to various recipients, view balances and statements.

2.4.1 Benefits of internet banking

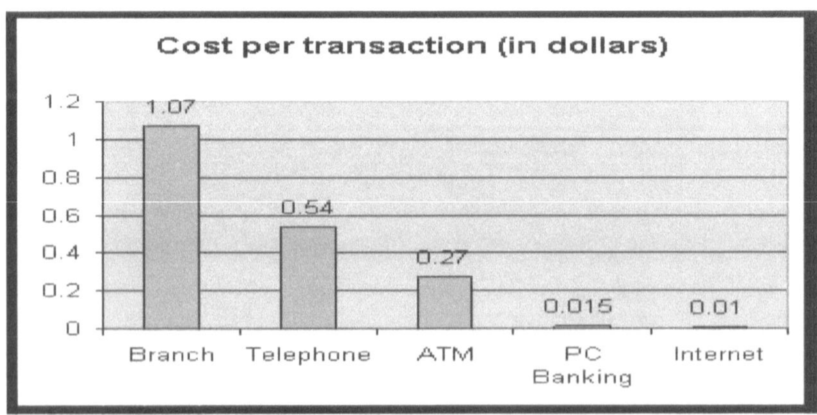

Figure 2.1: Advantage of internet banking in terms of banking cost, Source: Singh 2004

Internet or online banking result in a high reduction of banking costs due to no infrastructural required from the banks' side to house large number of customers to receive banking services. Traditionally banks have to maintain large infrastructures and many employees required to serve customers. E- Banking offers banking platform that allows accessibility to banking network from any location and perform necessary banking activities such as transfers and reception of money and account status viewing. The figure above indicates the trend in reduction of banking costs from traditional branches to internet banking in terms of US dollars in Indian bank. Using a branch for banking client needs to pay $1.07 to only $1.01 per transaction (Singh, 2004).

2.4.2 Recent trend in the uses of internet and internet banking

By the beginning of the 1990's few customers have not realized the benefit of internet and represented little significance to individuals and businesses. It has started from the humble beginning with majority of the users had no clear understanding of its characteristic. According to (UNCTD, 2003) the number of internet users reached 591 million worldwide by year 2020, with developing countries accounting for 32 percent while North America and Europe has 89 percent of the world internet hosts. On the bandwidth capacity Africa still lag behind with 20 times by Europe while North America leads Europe 8.4 times in terms of bandwidth capacity.

2.4.3 Current global internet usage 2000 to 2017

Table 2.1: World Internet usage (2000 - 2017)

World Regions	Population (2008 Est.)	Internet Users (Dec -2017)	Penetration (% Pop.)	Growth (2008 -2018)	Users of internet %
Africa	1,287,914,329	453 329 534	35%	9941%	11%
Asia	4 207 588 157	2 023 630 194	48%	1670%	49%
Europe	827 650 849	704 833 752	85%	570%	17%
Latin America/ Carib.	652 047 996	437 001 277	67%	2318%	11%
Middle East	254 438 981	164 037 259	65%	4893%	4%
North America	363 844 662	345 660 847	95%	219%	8%
Oceania / Australia	41 273 454	28 439 277	69%	273%	1%
WORLD TOTAL	7 634 758 428	4 156 932 140	54%	1052%	100%

Source: Internet World Statistic

The table above shows the trend and growth in usage of internet world wide over the past decade from the year 2000 to 2018. The number of users has grown from 360 million in year 2000 to 4 billion in year 2017. Africa users have grown from 4 million in year 2000 to 453 million in the year 2018, with largest percentage of growth among the continents of 1 052 percent which represent 54.4% penetration of the population.

The growth in the internet usage indicates the conversion from traditional banking to internet banking. The world economy has become ICT based economy, by lowering transaction cost, removal of long distance related barriers that has traditionally determined the location of service providers and good producers (UNCDT, 2003).

2.5   Concept of mobile phones and mobile banking

According to International Telecommunication Union, the subscribers of mobile phones worldwide reached 7.1 billion in 2015. However, 79% of the growths of subscribers are in the developing countries and the rest remains with developed countries. Traditionally mobile phones were invented for making calls to each other or sending messages. Over the past years, the potential for better uses of the mobile phones developed and characterised in other forms of economic enhancement through transactions between buyers and suppliers. There is a strong positive relationship with the number of mobile subscribes with the rate of economic growth. According to UNCTAD (2005) the economic benefits seen in the developing countries is a clear testimony of the growth of the mobile phone users in those countries.

2.5.1   Mobile banking channels

The delivery of mobile banking services to consumers involves the participation of four primary players; A Bank, Mobile Network Operator (MNO), a Mobile Banking Technology Vendor, and the consumer. The industry has been in the existence for many years but the potential beyond the basic functionality was not realised. According to Mobile Banking Technology Options (2007) the consumer mobile market has matured over the past years and consumers has realised the value proposition and hence bank and MNO has experienced high penetration of mobile phone users in their customer base. Mobile banking channel allows banks to deliver the services to customers at lower cost because there are no infrastructural costs. Mobile banking is operated in the virtual bank whereby customers can operate banking activities on their mobile handset with banking features embedded in the mobile phone menu. This channel is possible with the mobile operator network internet data connection. The new channel of mobile phone banking provides additional revenues to bank by identifying the new market segment that it cannot reach with the current channels of branches, ATM and point of sales. It also creates revenue for the MNO from the non-core business segment through the enabling channel of mobile banking provision.

2.5.2   The role of bank and MNO in mobile banking delivery

Banks does not deliver banking service to consumer independently; it requires the support of the mobile network operator. Banks hold a financial licence and processing capability required for the delivery of the banking services but get   infrastructural support from mobile operator necessary for final transmission of such service (Kruger, 2007). Banks and mobile network operator form technical partnership that allows them to work in tandem to reach the mobile consumer. The two partners form a mobile banking vendor between them that deliver the service mobile consumer by integrating the technicality of the bank with mobile network operator.

2.5.3   Benefits of Mobile banking

Mobile banking offers many benefits to banks and their customers. The main benefits are provision of better services to customers, cost effective channels, creating loyal customers, offering additional services, generating profit and holding up high- profit customers, efficiency and enhancement of bank's reputation and better customer service and satisfaction (Alalwan et al, 2015). The factors will be thoroughly elaborated here under.

2.5.4   Benefits to Mobile Network Operator

Mobile Network Operator has seen increased subscriptions in the intake of their services especially in developing countries over the year due to the incorporation of mobile banking channel in their portfolio. Large population in the developing countries has not been banked due to huge infrastructure requirement. Report by UNCTAD (2005) indicated that the increased subscription in the mobile network operator's customer base is relevant to the need of banking by the population that was not catered for by banks. Mobile banking aspiration by subscribes is a factor in the increases of subscription especially the micro – entrepreneurs.

2.5.5   Benefits to Banks

2.5.5.1 Options of multi-channel banking

Mobile banking offers banks multi-channel of banking service delivery by creating an additional customer segment that expand to the traditional channel and create additional source of income. The new banking channel is carried out at an efficient level in relation to the old one because it offers relieve and easiness to banking structure due to the absence of physical interaction with the customers.

2.5.5.2 Reduction in cost

Mobile banking is carried at lower transactional cost relative to traditional banking channel. ''Banks are embarking on migration strategy whereby moving their customer away from the more fixed – cost based infrastructure, such as branches to those with less resources and operational costs such ATMs, POS and ultimately internet and mobile banking'' (Kruger, 2007). Banks does not need to erect huge capital infrastructure to conduct the operation but require only the interaction system through its existing operating centre. The client are not required to visit the branches to conduct their normal transaction banking otherwise there are operating challenges regarding the accessibility of the services, thus requires the bank not to hold many personnel in the branches.

2.5.5.3   Market segmentation

Mobile subscribers segment presented bank with the market of banking. The bank has to formulate specific strategy to penetrate the mobile subscribes market with introduction of appealing features. The strategy has to identify the target market and the kind of mobile devices they use and the experience the users have to operate such devices. Kruger, (2007), argue that the more innovative, capable handset the target market have, the easy the bank to penetrate the market due to easiness of uses.

The target market should have access to the bearer channel that has relative low transaction cost and more affordable to the target market and has risk profile secured sufficiently. Security concern plays a vital role in the bank to select the channel due to inherent reputational bank risk if the channel happens to be breached and loose customer's money. The channel should be in compliances with all the guiding financial regulation and processing rules such as authentication of the customers, transfer of data and the level of encryption.

2.5.5.4   Benefits to consumer

Consumer has significant benefits in using mobile banking technology varying from the provision of better services, simplified consumer banking transaction (Adesuyi et al, 2013), reduction in costs, reap efficiency synergies to their businesses, access to wide variety of banking services from any location such as account transfers, money deposits and virtual payment completion (Gu et al, 2009). The above mentioned benefits are explained in details here under here.

2.5.5.5 Transaction cost savings,

Costs of transaction for making payments to suppliers, receipts from customers, withdrawals of cash inside the branch and at automated telling machines makes up the large portion of fees that customers pays to the bank each month. According to the pricing guide manual of First National Bank of Namibia, the cost of making a transfer between two accounts within the bank is N$60.00 inside the branch or check payment, over the counter while it is cost N$10.00 if mobile banking channel has been used (FNB Namibia 2017) While at Nedbank, most mobile transactions are free comparing to N$200.00 charged over the counter (Nedbank Namibia 2018) Mobile banking offers significant of cost savings that can be used to boost the operation of other areas of the business.

2.5.5.6 Efficiency

The mobile channel allows the customers to spend most of their time and concentrate on their businesses. Clients can switch on their mobile phones, access their banking channel and effect payments to suppliers, receive payment from their debtors, pay salaries from office and view balances and transactions. Customer can utilize this time to add value to their work and businesses. The cost of processing a transaction via mobile phone can be as much as 10 times lower than via an ATM and as much as 50 times lower than via a branch (Deloitte 2010).

2.5.5.7 Comfort

Mobile banking offers peace of mind and relaxation to customers by accessing the banking platform throughout the day provided that the location is covered by the mobile network operator. It is very fast, secure and efficient service. It offers up instant information on the status of the client's bank accounts.

2.6   Internet banking in Africa

The users of internet have grown fast from 2000 to 2017, from 4.5 million in the year 2000 to 453.3 million users in 2017. It represents a percentage growth of 9973% and 35.2% percent penetration rate each year (Internet World Statistic, 2018). The penetration of internet in Africa stems from the focus of development for economic independent. Development of ICT infrastructure and progression create competitive advantage in terms of trading and enhance the ability to compete for the economic share in the global market. In the past five years Africa has seen a high internet growth more than other continents but was second lowest on penetration (UNCDT, 2006). Nigeria, Egypt, Kenya and South Africa, account for 42% share in internet users.

Internet access is more universal nowadays with almost 100 percent connection in the large companies. There is still a huge challenge to penetrate the whole sector especially the SME's sector. Most financial sector has connection to internet and diversifying their offering in the internet channel, and has embarked on the mobilisation of customers to convert to internet channel of business. Among African countries South Africa, Kenya, Egypt, Morocco and Nigeria have the highest subscribers of internet.

2.7   Mobile banking in Africa

Internet connection in Africa has been on increase trend however it did not penetrate the wider market that would enable the entire population to access the banking channel. Only 1% of the African populations was connected to internet by 2005 and can access the banking channel (Porteous, 2006). The introduction of mobile banking has come at the right time at which the developing countries needed the wider participation of the citizens in the economy. Africa has seen significant strides in the increase in number of mobile network operator subscription, potentially driven by the need for banking channel over the wider area of mass market, Kruger, (2007) the increased usage of cell phone in Africa has driven the banks to pioneer with major MNO through banking collaboration entities such as MTN Banking, Globe, Smart, Celpay and Wizzit Bank as a leading innovators to use technology to expand the accessibility of financial services

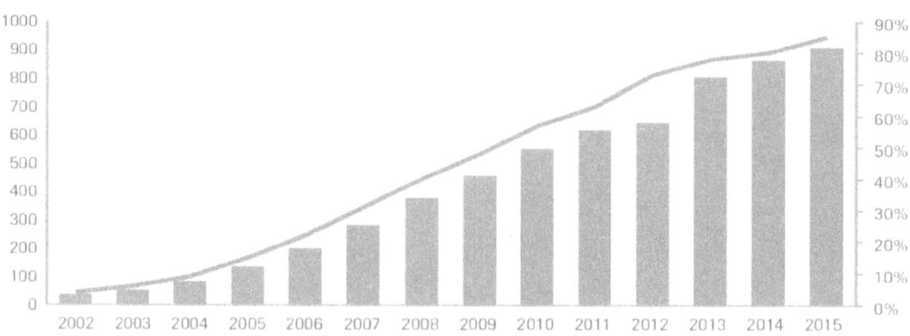

Figure 2.2 Mobile subscribers and penetration in AfricaSource: GSMA African observatory report.

The growth in mobile population in Africa stood at 2% in 2000 however it grew to more than 57% in 2010. This was a land-mark year for Africa as mobile penetration passed 50% for the first time. In lieu of the recorded growth over the year Africa requires investment in information technology infrastructure to harness the potential the continent possess and connect the remaining population.

Table 2.2: Mobile cellular telephone subscriptions (post – paid and prepaid) in millions and penetration rate as at 2016

Country	2003 (millions)	2017 (millions)	Penetration rate (%)
Angola	0.35	9	34
Botswana	0.45	1.6	69
Kenya	1.59	28.3	59
Namibia	0.22	1.2	45
South Africa	16.86	37.5	68
Zambia	0.24	9	53
Zimbabwe	0.36	9.4	58

Source: The mobile economy Sub – Saharan Africa 2017.

The selected countries in the SADC region with exceptions of Kenya have experienced a robust increase in the take up of mobile phone usage at 2017. The increase in penetration rate range from as low as 34 percent in Angola to high as 68 percent in South Africa. South Africa, Botswana and Kenya has seen an exponential growth in subscription and can be attributable to M-PESA mobile payment in Kenya and Wallet a Standard Bank and FNB products, Wizzit,

MTN banking, Flash mobile and Vodacom - Nedbank that enables the wider participation of rural population who had no opportunity to have access to banking channels.(Ondienge, 2010)

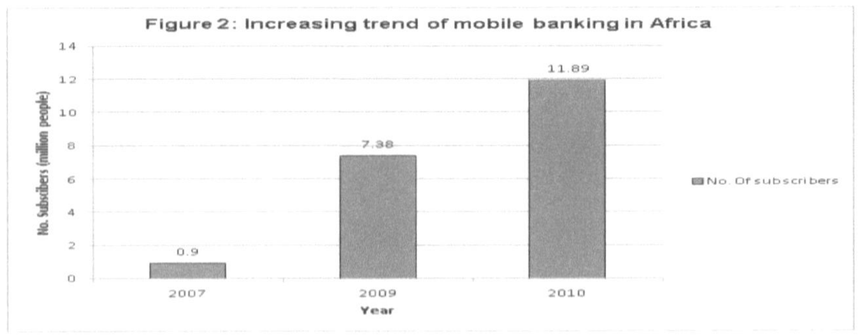

Figure 2.3: Increased trend of mobile banking in Africa: Source: AFDB

2.8   Mobile banking and payments in Kenya

As per Africa development bank report (Dec, 2010), Kenya is one of the country in Africa that demonstrated the success of integrating the rural population in the mainstream of the economy with the accessibility to the formal banking channel of the population that was not able to do so in the past. Before the introduction of Mobile Money scheme, only 19 percent of adult population had access to formal bank account and has been largely restricted to urban population (Mas, and Radcliffe, 2010). Cellular operator introduced M-Pesa, M-Kesho by Safricom and ZAP by Zain to introduce the extended mobile banking channel apart from the traditional branch banking. The number of mobile telephony which stood at 17.4 million in 2009 grew to 39.0 million in 2016 (Communication Authority of Kenya, 2016). Safaricom M-Pesa was formed in 2007 with 20 000 customers now has 16 million customers in 2016, which is about 56 percent of Kenya mobile population and The mobile phone is also the preferred mode of savings in the country, with 60% of Kenyans having their savings in services such as M-PESA, M-Shwari and KCB M-PESA" (Africa Business Communities 2018).

2.9　Mobile and internet banking in South Africa

2.9.1　Overview of South Africa

Electronic banking particularly internet in South Africa has penetrated most sectors of the economy with most banking and financial institutions offering e-banking services. The estimated cost reduced for using internet banking is 11 times of the traditional banking (Institute of Bankers, 2018).

Namibia is characterised with an almost similar financial and banking environment like in South Africa of which new trend of banking are imported from, especially the technological banking. The major banks in Namibia namely First National Bank, Standard Bank and Nedbank are subsidies of parent banks in South Africa, of which all of them are headquartered in South Africa. Mobile subscribers in South Africa per 100 people have reached 142.38 while the users of internet per 100 people have increased 28.5 million in 2016 (World Bank data 2016). It is interesting to note that most people in South Africa uses their mobile phone to access internet making the mobile subscriptions to surpass an amount 92.1 million subscribers at the end of 2017. The main contributor to internet usage was the introduction and uses of smart phones (ECN 2018).

2.9.2　Internet and mobile banking users in South Africa

The uses of internet in South Africa stand at 28.5 million in 2016, a growth of 533% from merely 4.5 million in 2008. Sahul Mungar, the Head of Marketing for digital banking at FNB, reiterated that around 1.5 million active devices in South Africa uses the FNB Banking App to access the online banking facilities at FNB. This indicates that many South African are migrating their over the counter banking to mobile applications, says a financial institution. Similar to Namibia, a larger number of small and medium business in South Africa makes up a larger number of the business operator and are not catered for by the newly introduced technological banking system. According to worldwideworx only a fraction of SME business operators find it very difficult to use complex technologies such as digital solutions and e-banking application due to limited understanding. Among all factors, one pertinent issue highlighted was the basic understanding to the inherent value and benefits associated with the benefits the mobile and wireless technology bring into the business hence their hesitation to test the new banking technology. Corporate businesses in South Africa has been embracing e-banking technology at a rapidly increasing pace however SME operators are left behind as the options become too complex and the choice too bewildering," (Goldstuck 2018).

2.10   Internet and mobile banking in Namibia

2.10.1 Overview of Namibia

Namibia borders with South Africa, Botswana, Zimbabwe, Zambia and Angola. It is a member of SADC economic and political block of the southern African countries. Namibia's economic size stood at USD27.02 billion at estimated purchasing power parity of 2017. The country has an official unemployment rate of 28.1 percent in 2016 with its population living below poverty line at 28.7 percent.

Due to lack of employment opportunities the notion of entrepreneurship is encouraged for those able to open new businesses to create employment opportunities for the unemployed mostly the youth. The economy is mostly supported by the export natural resources in a raw form such as diamond, uranium, copper, zinc, as well as agricultural and fisheries products such as beef and fisheries products.(World Fact Book, 2018). Namibian economic and financial activities are aligned and linked to South Africa's economy with the Namibian dollar pegged to South African rand.

2.10.2 Financial and banking market in Namibia

The financial market and more particularly the banking sector in Namibia is stable and well matured. The sector is dominated by four major banks First National bank, Standard bank, Bank Windhoek and Nedbank. These banks are all South African owned with exception of Bank Windhoek which has local ownership. The financial industry comprises of other players which cater for different products and services.

The different players are Namibia Post Limited which comprises in specialized transactional and savings banking apart from their core activities of freight mail and services. The other players in the banking sectors are Development Bank of Namibia which is a development financial institution which cater for SME and corporate loans. Other players such as Letshego Bank Namibia was recently granted a banking licence to diversify its operation from lending of personal loans to general transactional banking. The banks are well and soundly managed with wide sector capital adequacy ratio of 10 percent as at the end of 2017. Namibian bank reflect one of the high banking fees in the Southern Africa and this is as a result of the low population translating to small market condensed in few elite and these charges are compounded by the need for growth and future sustainability (IMF, 2007). All the four commercial banks with exception of the Namibia Post Limited offer specialized and innovative services such as web presence, internet and mobile banking. All Banks in Namibia have partnership with MNO and offer Wallet product.

2.10.4 The role and importance of SMEs in economic development

2.10.4.1 Definition of SME in Namibia

Small and medium Enterprises have been defined based on the different jurisdiction and economies. The definition in many countries are set out according to the activities and financial results of their business such as number of employees, sales, assets and turnover (BON, 2010).

Table 2.4: World Bank SME Definitions

Firm Size	Employees	Assets	or	Annual sales
Medium	< 200	< $ 15 million		< $ 15 million
Small	< 50	< $ 3 million		< $ 3 million
Micro	< 10	< $ 100 000		< $ 2 million

Source: Bank of Namibia

The World Bank defines the SME on the composition of number of employees, asset size and annual sales turnover, and also on series of loan size ranges as a proxy definition for the micro, small and medium client segments (Bon, 2010).

Table 2.5: Ministry of Industrialisation in Namibia SME Definition:

Sector	Employment	Turnover (N$)	Capital Employed (N$)
Manufacturing	Fewer than 10 persons	1 000 000	500 000
Service	Fewer than 5 persons	250 000	100 000

Source: Larri and Nepru/ Bank of Namibia

The Ministry of Industrialisation and SME Development in Namibia defines SME based on the scope of work. The scope of work distinct whether the SME business operator is in the service or manufacturing business of which an SME category is formed. This make the definition to become difficult to measure because some parameters such as capital investment due to the impact of inflation, however the number of employees is simple to measure and it's a valid criteria normally used (BoN, 2010). Small and Medium Enterprises in Namibia conduct their business across all range of products and services in all economic sector. Numbers of SME companies were created in the construction sector during the economic boom between the years 2008 to 2015, mostly driven by increased government expenditure.

2.10.4.2   The role of the SME's in the economy

The small and medium enterprises sector are deemed as the backbone of most economy due to the ability to create employment opportunities most specifically in developing economies such as Namibia (Arnold et al, 2005). The Namibian economy is made up of small number of corporate businesses who are the major contributor to the economic growth and employer of the fraction of population mostly the educated graduates being second from the government. The SME sector complement the other role players such as the government and corporate businesses in driving the economic growth in most developing countries by contributing to socio economic development most particularly in employment creation for semi and non-skilled population. The Namibian government has been stimulating the economy with targeted intervention programme economic growth through creation of temporary projects such as housing and infrastructure development on the low scale level.

2.10.4.3   Internet and mobile subscriptions in Namibia

World Bank report (2016) indicates Namibia has 392 181 internet users representing 15.6 percent of the total at the end of 2016. The users reported are those accessing the internet from worldwide network. The internet subscription has been slowly growing having been at average 5.63% percent since 2010. The number represent low subscription of internet access given the country high GDP per capita in Africa that is characterised by uneven distribution of income. Mobile cell phone subscriptions have reached an amount of 2.66 million users in 2016 from 0.61 million in 2006. The amount represent 105 percent of the population has an access to mobile technology, and a 100.683 per 100 people (World Bank data, 2018).

2.11 Empirical Literature: Behavioural intention to use internet and mobile banking

In order to grasp the reasons of SME behavioral electronic banking usage, studies conducted advises the uses of inclusive theoretical model which appropriately fit to assess the adoption intention, this model is UTAUT theory (Tai and Ku, 2013).
The UTAUT model was developed to offer a cross-validated framework that explains an individual's intention to adopt new technologies across various organizational and societal contexts (Celik, 2016).

The UTAUT used in this study is a product of eight Technology Acceptance Models and theories of reasoned action, TAM/TAM2, motivation model, theory of planned behavior, combined TAM and TPB, model of PC utilization, innovation diffusion theory and social cognitive theory (Venkatesh et al., 2003). Wong and Huang, (2011) further stated that these theories mentioned by Venkatesh combines the psychological and behavioral theories and complement each other by combining their variables into each other and harness them to provide empirically support model to enable a thorough examination of all core determinants of technology adoption intention by the researchers.

Yu, (2012) indicates that UTAUT holds greater statistical and explanatory power while Yu 2012 further added that many studies have broadly used TAM theory however this theory comes short to UTAUT because it can predict only 40 percent usage intention while the UTAUT theory can explains 70 percent of electronic banking usage.

UTAUT2 is an improvement from the original UTAUT which consist of four variables that dictates the individuals' impact on technology acceptance and their overall intention to adopt it. These variables are performance expectancy, effort expectancy, social influence and facilitating conditions (Venkatesh et al., 2003). Improving on UTAUT2 theory three new variables were added which are habit, hedonic motivation and price sensitivity/value or perceived value (Kumar et al., 2012; Venkatesh et al., 2012; Baptista and Oliveira, 2016). UTAUT2 indeed possess greater strength because it includes hedonic variables in addition to the utilitarian constructs which are addressed in the original UTAUT (Lua et al., 2016).

Performance expectancy and e- banking

Performance expectancy is the first factor in UTAUT theory, which predict that the SME will believe in the usage of a certain technology if it will enhance the business performance through perceived usefulness, external motivation, outcome expectations, comparative advantage and job fit (Tai and Ku, 2013). Chiao-Chen, (2013) further posited that this variable reflects an SME awareness of the banking technology that it enhances value propositions in products and services in terms of performance whether in the form of efficiency, accessibility, and customer and supplier response rate.

Performance expectancy therefore drives consumer/SME to adopt e-banking services through perception that the banking technology services will expedite, simplify and enhance their banking transactions when compared to old way of banking (Tan and Lau, 2016).

Effort expectancy and e-banking

Effort expectancy deals with the level of easiness to operate the internet and mobile technology (Yu, 2012). It indicates the amount of effort required to study and learn how to use such technology (Tai and Ku, 2013). An SME in all likelihood will adopt the service if they assume it is easy to use those applications with little effort (Park et al., 2007), especially in the case of self-service technologies, such as e-banking, which requires consumers to complete their transactions independent of any assistance (Alalwan et al., 2015).

Social influence and e-banking

Social influence variable deals with SME's perception that important people in his or her life uses and think that he/she also should start using e-banking technology (Yu, 2012). This construct is based and founded upon the concepts of subjective norms and social image of which an SME is expected to likely adopt behaviors selected and accepted by his or her business peers and important others (Tan et al., 2010; Mbrokoh, 2016). Various studies have evidenced that what the society expect is normally influenced by the subjective norms when it concerns an individual's behavioral intentions to adopt a technology (Farah, 2017a), therefore this expectation guide the individual belief and behavior while also allaying doubt and fears regarding the adoption of a new service (Illia et al., 2015). This view has been confirmed to be true by Yu, (2012) especially in the case of mobile applications, which have becomes so pertinent on the online social network, thus enhancing the impact of important others' opinions.

Facilitating condition and e-banking

Facilitating condition variable informs that the users of e –banking technology perceive the extent to which environmental factors both internal and external are greater than the barriers to adopt the technology which helps in the acceptance of new technologies (Nel et al., 2012). The factors that promote the adoption of given behaviours are mostly the availability and accessibility of resources (Siddik et al., 2014). There is always a likelihood that SME will adopt e-banking services if the financial resources are available combined with the necessary skills required to operate these services and a working network (Chemingui and Hajer, 2013).

Habit and e-banking

Moorthy et al, (2017) Argue that most researchers have concluded due to the impact to consumer's intentions and preferences, habit is one of the strong barriers to new technology adoption. Habit is the extent to which an SME carry out a certain behavior automatically and repetitively based on experience and knowledge acquired over time (Alalwan et al., 2015). An SME is unlikely to change an obtained habit and, therefore, is likely to resist any new and unfamiliar interactions with his/her bank (Chemingui and Hajer, 2013); this normally generates consumer hesitation to adopt new applications and services such as e-banking (Antón et al., 2013). In fact, past experience and habit tend to become an unconscious element that can significantly inhibit consumers' willingness to learn new methods because their decision making are relied on past experience instead of utilizing cognitive reasoning (Venkatesh et al., 2016; Zhang et al., 2017). Similarly, consumers who utilize offline banking are familiar with those habits and abilities required hence so challenging to develop and adopt new ways of e-banking (Hanafizadeh et al., 2013).

Hedonic motivation and e-banking

Hedonic motivation variable in UTAUT2 informs the level of pleasure and joy a consumer gains from using a technology (Brown and Venkatesh, 2005). Hedonic deals with emotions and its impulses are non-functional and based on an individual's affective needs (Malik et al., 2013). The pleasure and enjoyment derived from using a new technology plays a significant role in enhancing a consumer's adoption intentions (Alalwan et al., 2015).

Curran and Meuter (2007) indicated that hedonic motives tend to be major determinants in a consumer's likelihood to adopt self-service technologies.

Perceived value and e-banking

 Perceived value or price sensitivity is the degree of price elasticity when using electronic banking (Venkatesh et al, 2012). Although most e-banking services and applications are free most study on e-banking has replaced the price value or sensitivity with perceived value gained from the usage of e-banking services (Streeter, 2009; Al-Jabri and Sohail, 2012) and incorporates both monetary and non-monetary value allowing for a more broad analysis (Gao and Bai, 2014).

Perceived value is a SMEs evaluation of a service/ product's overall worth by comparing its expected benefits vs its expected costs (Zhu et al., 2010). The perceived value of e-banking applications includes a consumer's subjective perception of the application's utilitarian and hedonic advantages and this includes its functionality, enjoyment, interactivity, accessibility, service quality and overall usefulness (Arcand et al., 2017). A consumer is likely to adopt a technology that maximizes subjective value and presents him/her with the greatest advantages (Dootson et al., 2016).

Venkatesh et al. (2003) provided an insight and approach to the adoption of internet technology adoption specifically the electronic banking with comprehensive, culturally and empirical tested set of variables. The model takes into account the sensitivity that is perceived as generic part into the uses of the technology. UTAUT provides flexibility for the dependent variables that affect the independent variable to be contextualised and address the aim of the research. It allows attitudes of the electronic banking users to be explained independently from the whole banking concepts and without the influence of other variables.

CHAPTER 3

Research methodology

3.1   Introduction

This section will describe and explain how the research is designed and the methods utilised to carry out the study. The study has used structured questionnaires formulated according to the Unified Theory of Acceptance and Use of Technology (UTAUT), using both qualitative and quantitative methods to assess the behaviour and awareness of internet and mobile banking among the small and medium business operator more particularly indicating the factors that hinders the adoption of the new e-banking technology in this business sector. The researcher has selected three towns in Namibia, Oshakati, Outapi and Otjiwarongo to represent the whole SME population in Namibia. The towns were selected due to the level of understanding and exposure of the SME population in each town namely Otjiwarongo is rated to have more educated and exposed SMEs followed by Oshakati and then Outapi. Trustworthiness is a key point in this study and was discussed in depth with each respondent to ensure scientific value of the study.

3.2   Research design

Chinn & Krammer, (1991), Mouton, (1996) & Babbie & Mouton, (2001) describes the research design as a strategy, logical instruction and set of guidelines that the researcher should consistently follow to address the research problem. The logic in using a research design in the study is to assist the researcher to maximise the validity of the research result by minimising errors through the anticipation of appropriate research decisions.

3.2.1 Quantitative design

A quantitative design is a systematic, objective and a formal, process which aims to test and describe the relationship between variables in the research (Burns & Grove 1993). Research design is defined as the strategy and logical process to be followed to enable the researcher to answer the research problem (Mouton 1996). Quantitative design in this study will help the researcher with understanding of factors causing the SME business operator not to adopt internet and mobile banking and propose how these challenges can be improved.

3.2.2   Population and Sampling

Population is the whole sets of individuals having similar characteristic (Pilot & Hungler, 1996). Sullivan and Russel (1995) explained population as a set of unity, in which the investigator is interested, that is the larger set from which the sample is drawn. The population for this study consists of all of small and medium enterprises business operators based in Namibia which use electronic banking services. From the population SMEs, a sample size of 200 was selected through a random sampling at the convenience of the researcher due to limitations.

3.3   Data collection

Data collection is the precise, systematic gathering of information which is relevant to the research purposes and specific objectives (Burns & Grove, 1993). The data collected from the two northern towns of Oshakati and Outapi for two weeks while the researcher took one week to collect data from the central north town of Otjiwarongo. The two northern towns were chosen on the basis of having semi – educated SMEs while Otjiwarongo consists more exposed SMEs due to the educational history of the country. The researcher collected the data personally using structured questionnaires at SME's parks around the three towns. The questionnaire consist two similar questions following each other for internet and mobile banking per respondent. Each questionnaire lasted 15 – 20 minutes and the whole exercise took one month.

3.4   Reliability

The research took four weeks to complete the entire data collection process, allocating three weeks to two towns in the far north Oshakati and Outapi while one week was allocated to the town of Otjiwarongo. The two towns in the far north were considered to have semi-educated SMEs hence the allocation of more time than the town in the central north, thus reliability coefficients were moderate to higher for such shorter period of time and each respondent has only one chance to administer and complete the questionnaire. Items on the likert rating scale were 28 questions for internet and mobile banking and the split half technique has been applied by distributing the same questionnaire to the SMEs completed in the presence of the researcher. This was done to ensure internal consistency of the data collected. The odds items are measuring the same attribute as the even items ensure internal consistency (Pilot & Hungler, 1991).

3.5 Validity

To maintain content validity, the scale used in this study was adapted from academically validated scales (Glavee-Geo et al., 2017). The study used Likert scale to better fit the context of this study to examine the SME's behavioral intention to adopt and actual usage of internet and mobile banking.

3.6 Data Analysis

3.6.1 Multiple regression model

The model was used to examine the relationship between the predictors which are independent variables and dependent variables which are based to the UTAUT2 model. It will also be used to examine and determine the relationship between the behaviour for intention and the actual use of internet and mobile banking by the small and medium enterprises in Namibia.

The seven predictors which are performance expectancy, effort expectancy, social influence, facilitating condition, hedonic motivation, perceived value and habit moderated by age, gender and experience are anticipated to have an influence on behavioural intentions to use e-banking. The general formula of a multiple regression model for the population will interpret the results binary logistic model and looks as follow.

$$Y_i = \beta_0 + \beta_1 X1_i + \beta_2 X2_i + \cdots \ldots + \beta_k XK_i + \varepsilon \ldots\ldots\ldots\ldots\ldots\ldots\ldots\ldots 1$$

Where: Y is the dependent variable xk are the predictors
$\beta 0$ = Regression constant of the population; βi=Regression coefficient for each variable of the population xi; =1, 2,…k, ε= Error term

The regression for the determinants of behavioural intention to use electronic banking is specified in equation 1;

$$BI_i = \beta_0 + \beta_1 PE_i + \beta_2 EE_i + \beta_3 SI_i + \beta_4 FC_i + \beta_5 HM_i + \beta_6 PV_i + \beta_7 HT_i + \beta_8 ATUT_i + \beta_9 X_i + \varepsilon_i$$
$$\ldots\ldots\ldots\ldots\ldots\ldots\ldots\ldots\ldots\ldots\ldots\ldots\ldots 1$$

Where BI_i is Behavioural Intention of respondent i to use electronic banking, which is categorized into internet banking and mobile banking; PE_i denotes performance expectancy of respondents$i$; EE_i refers to effort expectancy; SIi refer to social influence on respondent; FCi refers to facilitating conditions by respondents, HM$_i$ refer to hedonic motivation by respondents, PVim denotes price value by the respondents, HT$_i$ refers to habit of the respondents while ATUT denotes the behavioural intention impact on user technology. X denotes a vector of demographic variables made up of age, gender, occupation, experience and education. In addition, the study also examined the electronic banking usage behaviour.

The user behaviour is defined as respondent usage of internet and mobile banking (internet and mobile banking) or otherwise, which is specified in equation 2;

$$UB_i = \beta_0 + \beta_1 PE_i + \beta_2 EE_i + \beta_3 SI_i + \beta_4 FC_i + \beta_5 HM_i + \beta_6 PV_i + \beta_7 HT_i + \beta_8 ATUT_i + \beta_9 X_i +$$
$$\varepsilon_i \dots\dots\dots\dots\dots\dots\dots\dots\dots\dots\dots 2$$

Where UB_i is the electronic banking usage behaviour of respondent I, defined as 1 if respondent uses either internet banking or mobile banking and zero otherwise. All other the variables are as defined before.

3.6.2   Dependent Variables

3.6.2.1 Behavioural intention (BI) and Usage Behaviour

The two dependent variables used in this study are behavioural intention and usage behaviour of electronic banking defined as internet banking and mobile banking. Behavioural intention in this context represent the will of the respondents (SMEs) to carry out an act and implement a certain behavior for future actual use. In this study, behavioural intention is defined as measure of the strength of a SME's intention to use internet banking and mobile banking. The behavioural intention to adopt were measured using a three-item scale adopted from Venkatesh et al. (2003) on five-point Likert scale. The second dependent variable is the actual usage behaviour of internet and mobile banking in Namibia by SMEs. The electronic banking user behaviour (EBU) is a categorical variable measured as 1 if an SME uses either internet or mobile banking and zero otherwise.

3.6.3 Independent Variables:

In this research, the variables in the UTAUT2 model of Venkatesh et al. (2012) as adopted Farah et al. (2018) are employed as the explanatory factors of behavioural intention to use internet and mobile banking. The seven constructs are explained below.

3.6.1.1 Performance expectancy (PE)

This factor provide useful functionality in the life of the business. It is the driver of behavioral intention to adopt the electronic banking (Dwivedi et al, 2017). The user feels that the banking technology enhances the business processes in regards to customers and suppliers alike. It provide external business motivation in the form of image and brand building and strengthening. Performance expectancy enhance and harmonise relationship among the SMEs themselves in terms of self-trading and build confidence and trust in the exchange of good and services especially at the SME Parks where most of them operates from. This factor is expected to have a positive effect on behavioural intention to use internet and mobile banking. This construct is measured using four-item scale from Venkatesh et al. (2003), which assesses users' belief that internet and mobile banking will improve performance. The respondents were required to indicate agreement to the four-items on 5-point Likert scale.

3.6.1.2 Effort expectancy (EE)

This construct implies that if the new banking technologies in the SME context is easy to learn and use and also instruction clear, simple and understandable, the users will become skilful and use it more (Venkatesh et al, 2003). Zhou et al. 2010 and Venkatesh et al., 2012 in their previous research indicated that this variable is so important in determining the intention of SME customer to adopt electronic banking.

Venkatesh et al (2003) further implore that effort expectancy will have a positive impact on behavioural intention to use internet and mobile banking if the user become knowledgeable and skilful. This construct is measured using four-item scale from Venkatesh et al. (2003), which assesses users' belief that internet and mobile banking will improve the performance of their businesses. The SME were required to indicate agreement to the four-items on 5-point Likert scale.

3.6.1.3   Social influence (SI)

Social influence plays a role in the adoption of internet and mobile banking technology that the SME will be inclined to use it if the important peers and fellow SME business operators start or using it. Social influence has been significant in determining a SME intention to use new technology (Moore and Benbasat, 1991; Venkatesh et al., 1996; Thompson et al., 1991). There is a positive expectancy that SMEs in Namibia will be influenced corporate segment to use the electronic banking, hence expected to have a positive effect on behavioural intention to use internet and mobile banking. This construct is measured using four-item scale from Venkatesh et al. (2003), which assesses users' belief that internet and mobile banking will improve performance. The respondents were required to indicate agreement to the four-items on 5-point Likert scale.

3.6.1.4   Facilitating condition (FC)

Most people in Namibia including SMEs possess personal computers and mobile devices for other personal and business activities. Although these devices possess other features they are hardly used for banking purposes. Facilitating condition informs the extent the SME in Namibia have necessary resources including the connecting operating network. It is expected to have a positive effect on behavioural intention to use internet and mobile banking if all the necessary resources are in place. This construct is measured using four-item scale from Venkatesh et al. (2003), which assesses users' belief that internet and mobile banking will improve performance. The SMEs were required to indicate agreement to the four-items on 5-point Likert scale.

3.6.1.5   Hedonic motivation (HM)

Venketash et al, (2003) defines hedonic motivation as the degree the internet and mobile technology provide fun, joy and pleasure from using it. Curan and Meuter (2007) inform that intrinsic motivation plays an important role in adoption of E- banking. E-banking is expected to provide joy to the SME once they believes that e-banking technology improve the business functionality and easy to use. It is expected to have positive effect on behavioural intention to use internet and mobile banking. This construct is measured using four-item scale from Venkatesh et al. (2003), which assesses users' belief that internet and mobile banking will improve performance. The SMEs were required to indicate agreement to the four-items on 5-point Likert scale.

3.6.1.6   Perceived value (PV)

Venkatesh et al. (2003) implored that, the users of e-banking should derive value from the service by spending their income on acquisition of infrastructures such as laptop, PC and mobile device, and access to internet data etc. SMEs in Namibia cognitively compares the value they receive from using the e-banking services (Dodds et.al, 1991) are expected to be sensitive to spend their hard earned income on the devices and data that are perceived not to have value addition to their business hence the effect of the price to influence the behavioural intention to use electronic banking. It is expected to have a positive effect on behavioural intention to use internet and mobile banking if all the necessary costs are affordable and competitive. This construct is measured using four-item scale from Venkatesh et al. (2003), which assesses users' belief that internet and mobile banking will improve performance. The SMEs were required to indicate agreement to the four-items on 5-point Likert scale.

3.6.1.7   Habit (HT)

Kim and Malhotra. (2005) describe habit as prior behaviour while Lamayem et al. (2007) describe habit as an individual behaviour to be automatic. Habit defines the act of using the internet and mobile technology service repeatedly and without mental conscious awareness by the SME or any other users (Venkatesh et al, 2003). The SME are expected to lack fluency in using the internet and mobile banking due to seldom use of the banking applications. This factor is expected to have a positive effect on behavioural intention to use internet and mobile banking. This construct is measured using four-item scale from Venkatesh et al. (2003), which assesses users' belief that internet and mobile banking will improve performance. The SME were required to indicate agreement to the four-items on 5-point Likert scale.

3.7   Control Variables

Age, has influence on all the independent variables on behavioral intention and users behaviour such that the effect is more stronger for the younger users than the older users. Gender, has influence on all the independent variables on behavioral intention and users behaviour such that the effect is more stronger for women using electronic banking than men. Experience, has influence on all the independent variables on behavioral intention and users behaviour such that the effect is more stronger for more experienced users than the less experienced users. Education, has influence on all the independent variables on behavioral intention and users' behaviour such that the effect is more stronger for high educated users than those users with less educational exposure.

3.8   Estimation Framework

3.8.1   Confirmatory Factor Analysis: Validity and Reliability of Constructs

The study has used Confirmation Factor Analysis technique which is used to confirm the relationship of the constructs and respective factors of that constructs (Netemeyer et al. 2003). In contrary to other techniques, CFA allow the researcher to make differences between the models and determines the extent to which the alternative model explain the relationship between the items on the scale so that effective decision can be made about the validity of the targeted model (Thompson and Daniel, 1996). The researcher has used CFA to measure the validity of the questionnaires used in the study. The study also used Cronbach alpha and composite reliability to measure the internal consistency of all constructs (Bagozzi and Yi, 1988, Nunnally, 1978). Discriminant and convergent validity were analysed by measuring the square of correlation between factors, average variance extracted AVE measures the explained variance of the construct (Fornell & Larcker, 1981).

3.8.2   Regression Analysis (OLS and Logistic regression)

In this study a parametric statistical analysis technique ordinary least squares (OLS) has been used to assess the effect of multiple factors on one response measures. OLS models yield one parameters estimate and associated standard error per explanatory measure and thus provide representations of variable relationship (Denham, 2010). It may imply x and y relationship which may be linear even if one of the two factor does not exist. In the same context of the logistic regression technique was preferred instead of others to analyse multivariate normality and continuous data involving the independent and/or dependent variables. Logistic regression is useful analysis technique for the modelling and discrimination in electronic banking adoption. The model outcome variable are rather binary or dichotomous and the independent variables are continuous variable, categorical variable or both (Akinci et al, 2007).

3.9 Limitations

The study was limited only to three towns in Namibia hence the sample size was small to represent the entire population of the SMEs in the country. Two towns are least developed and lies in the rural settings of the country while one town is moderately developed and located in urban area. Although the researcher has anticipated this challenge, SMEs shares same behaviour and attitude on the uses of the e- banking. The following chapter will analyse and discuss the results of the study.

Chapter 4

Findings and Discussion

4.1   Introduction

This chapter will look into organising and giving meaning to the data collected by analysing, presenting and discuss the result of data. These results are based on the data collected from the SMEs by means of structured questionnaires that was issued and administered by the researcher. It also forms the background against which the appropriateness of the methods that were used could be judged (Burns & Groove, 1993 and Sapsford & Jupp, 1996).

4.2   Demographic profile and Descriptive statistics

Data was collected from the population of 200 SMEs with a sample size of n=132 SMEs from three towns, Outapi, Oshakati and Otjiwarongo. The researcher was able to collect 132 of the 200 questionnaires from the sample person representing (66%) that could respond while 68 (34%) did not take part at all. Hence the response rate was adequate and reliable. Among those who did not take part in the research included 46 (forty six) who brought incomplete questionnaires, 11 (eleven) brought blank questionnaires and 7 (seven) indicated not to understand them. One questionnaire consisting of two similar questions for internet and mobile banking was given to each respondent to complete and the demographic characteristic of the sample with its relative number of responses are presented in Table 4.1.

Table 4.1 Descriptive data

		Frequency	Percentage
Age	Below 19 years	3	2%
	20-29	35	27%
	30-39	54	41%
	40-49	28	21%
	50-59	9	7%
	above 60 years	3	2%
Gender	Male	60	45%
	Female	72	55%
Occupation	SME	98	74%
	Employed	31	23%
	Other	3	2%
Qualification	Below Grade 12	42	32%
	Grade 12	66	50%
	Above Grade 12	24	18%
Experience	1-5 Years	19	14%
	6-10 years	44	33%
	11-15years	38	29%
	16-20years	21	16%
	Above 20 years	10	8%
Internet Banking Usage	Yes	86	65%
	No	46	35%
Mobile Banking Usage	Yes	71	54%
	No	61	46%

Source: Author's generated output

The questionnaire consisted of six age categories for the participants in the study (19 and under, 20 -29, 30 – 39, 40 – 49, 50 – 59 and 60 and above). Table 4.1 present the age analysis as follows 54 (41%) of the respondents were in the age category of 30 – 39 years, 35 (27%) in 20 – 29 years, 28 (21%) were in 40 – 49 years, 9 (7%) were in 50 -59 years category while 3 (2%) were under and another 3 (2%) were 60 and over.

Gender of the respondents who took part in the study are shown in the table 4.1 above of which, 72 (55%) of the respondents were female while 60 (45%) were men. It is interesting to know that 98 (74%) were SME clients, 31 (23%) were employed and running SME businesses and 3 (3%) were others. Sixty six 66 (50%) of the respondents have grade 12, while 24 (18%) are have qualification above grade 12 and the remaining 42 (32%) of the respondents have below grade 12 qualification.

Experience has 5 different classes. Forty four 44 (33%) participants has 6 – 10 years of experience in business, 38 (29%) has 11 – 15 years, 21 (16%) has 16 – 20 years, 19 (14%) has 1 – 5 years while 10 (7%) has 21 and more years of experience in business. Among the respondents, 86 (65%) are currently using internet banking while 46 (35%) are not using the internet banking service. Similarly 71 (54%) of the respondents uses mobile banking while 61 (46%) does not make use of the service.

Table 4.2 presents the mean, standard deviation, minimum and maximum values for variables in the regression model for internet banking. On average behavioral intentions recorded high responses with a mean of 3.72 illustrating the interest of respondents in the uses of banking technology however facilitating conditions recorded highest variation of the responses. The second highest observation was habit with a mean of 3.44 indicating the average interest in the way toward changing of lifestyle in embracing the banking technology and unseating the old way of doing things. Similarly habit records a high variance of 1.51 equalling to its mean. Performance expectancy has the lowest responses with mean of 2.40 with a variation of 1.68 while price value recorded an average responses of 3.35 and a variation of 1.52. The remaining independent variables of effort expectancy, social influence facilitating conditions and hedonic motivation have an average response ranging from 3.04 to 3.43 with a variation of 1.23 to 1.72 from their means

Table 4.2: Descriptive statistics for internet banking

Factors	No of respondents	Min	Max	Mean	Std. Dev.	Variance
Performance Expectancy	132	1	5	2.40	1.298	1.686
Effort Expectancy	132	2	5	3.31	1.113	1.239
Social Influence	132	1	5	3.04	1.284	1.649
Facilitating Conditions	132	1	5	3.43	1.315	1.728
Perceived Value	132	1	5	3.35	1.236	1.526
Habit	132	1	5	3.44	1.231	1.515
Hedonic Motivation	132	1	5	3.33	1.227	1.506
Behavioural Intentions	132	1	5	3.72	1.200	1.440

Source: Author's generated output

Table 4.3 presents the mean, standard deviation, minimum and maximum values for variables in the regression model for mobile banking. On average social influence recorded high responses with a mean of 2.939 illustrating the interest of respondents in the uses of mobile banking technology based on the influence of the society however price value recorded highest variation of the responses. The second highest observation was effort expectancy with an average responses of 2.871 indicating the comfort and easy uses of the mobile banking technology. Similarly price value records a high variance of 1.318 followed by hedonic motivation. Behavioral intentions has the lowest responses with mean of 2.045 with a variation of 0.578 while performance expectancy recorded an average responses of 2.447 and a variation of 0.722. The remaining independent variables of facilitating conditions, hedonic motivation and habit have an average response ranging from 2.795 to 2.523 with a variation of 1.015 to 0.714 from their means

Table 4.3: Descriptive statistics for mobile banking

Factor	No of respondents	Min	Max	Mean	Std. Dev.	Variance
Performance expectancy	132	1	5	3.269	1.0492	1.101
Effort expectancy	132	1	5	3.121	1.1708	1.371
Social influence	132	1	5	2.910	1.1150	1.244
Facilitating condition	132	1	5	3.318	1.2514	1.566
Hedonic motivation	132	1	5	3.370	1.3450	1.808
Perceived value	132	1	5	3.470	1.2380	1.533
Habit	132	1	5	3.284	1.1141	1.241
Behavioural intention	132	1	5	3.670	1.1300	1.277

Source: Author's generated output

4.3 Measurement model and Reliability testing for mobile and internet banking

To ensure that the measurements were reliable and valid, the items and constructs for internet and mobile banking were examined for validity and reliability. As shown in Tables 4.4 and 4.5, the values for Cronbach's α and composite reliability (CR) are greater than 0.7, indicating good internal consistency of all the constructs. In addition, the loadings of the items on each construct was observed to the 0.50 threshold to indicate the high explanatory factors for the constructs. All constructs have average variance explained (AVE) values above the 0.50 threshold, indicating the items collectively explains more than 50% of the variations in the constructs.

Table 4.4: Convergent validity results internet banking

Measures	Factor loading	Cronbach's α	Composite Reliability	AVE
PERFORMANCE EXPECTANCY		0.941	0.827	0.548
I find internet banking useful in my business	0.617			
Using internet banking increases my chances of achieving things that are important to me	0.758			
Using internet banking helps me accomplish things more quickly	0.693			
Using internet banking increases productivity of my business	0.87			
EFFORT EXPECTANCY		0.975	0.928	0.764
Learning how to use internet banking is easy	0.832			
Instructions to use internet banking are clear and understandable	0.883			
I find internet banking easy to use	0.896			
It is easy for me to become skillful at using internet banking	0.885			
SOCIAL INFLUENCE		0.949	0.885	0.720
People who are important think that I must use internet banking	0.799			
People who influence my behaviour think that I should use internet banking	0.91			
People whose opinion I value prefer that I use internet banking	0.832			
FACILITATING CONDITION		0.978	0.911	0.720
I have resources necessary to use internet banking	0.756			
I have knowledge necessary to use internet banking	0.931			
Internet technology is similar to other technologies I use	0.918			
I can get help from others when I have difficulties using mobile banking	0.774			
HEDONIC MOTIVATION		0.973	0.934	0.825
Using internet technologies is fun	0.914			
Using internet technologies is enjoyable	0.922			
Using internet technologies is very entertaining	0.889			
PERCEIVED VALUE		0.957	0.892	0.734
It is very cheap to use internet banking then traditional banking	0.782			
PC internet is reasonably priced and offer good value for money	0.883			
At the current price, PC internet provides a good value	0.901			
HABIT		0.979	0.928	0.765
The use of internet banking has become a habit to me	0.921			
I am addicted to using internet banking	0.813			
I must use internet banking	0.915			
Using internet banking has become natural to me	0.844			
BEHAVIORAL INTENTION		0.969	0.927	0.809
I intend to continue using internet banking in the future	0.888			
I will always try to use internet banking every time I do my banking	0.865			
I plan to use internet banking more times	0.944			

Source: Author generated output

Table 4.5: Convergent validity results for mobile banking

Measures	Factor loading	Cronbach's α	Composite Reliability	AVE
PERFORMANCE EXPECTANCY		0.945	0.830	0.533
I find mobile banking useful in my business	0.66			
Using mobile banking increases my chances of achieving things that are important to me	0.76			
Using mobile banking helps me accomplish things more quickly	0.69			
Using mobile banking increases productivity of my business	0.849			
EFFORT EXPECTANCY		0.966	0.900	0.694
Learning how to use mobile banking is easy	0.718			
Instructions to use mobile banking are clear and understandable	0.845			
I find mobile banking easy to use	0.884			
It is easy for me to become skillful at using mobile banking	0.875			
SOCIAL INFLUENCE		0.946	0.852	0.657
People who are important think that I must use mobile banking	0.759			
People who influence my behaviour think that I should use mobile banking	0.877			
People whose opinion I value prefer that I use electronic banking	0.792			
FACILITATING CONDITION		0.981	0.921	0.747
I have resources necessary to use electronic banking	0.759			
I have knowledge necessary to use electronic banking	0.935			
Mobile and internet technology is similar to other technologies I use	0.903			
I can get help from others when I have difficulties using mobile and electronic banking	0.849			
HEDONIC MOTIVATION		0.971	0.933	0.822
Using mobile and internet technologies is fun	0.898			
Using mobile and internet technologies is enjoyable	0.929			
Using mobile and internet technologies is very entertaining	0.893			
PERCIEVED VALUE		0.969	0.901	0.753
It is very cheap to use mobile and internet banking then traditional banking	0.798			
Mobile and PC internet is reasonably priced and offer good value for money	0.943			
At the current price, mobile and PC internet provides a good value	0.856			
HABIT		0.976	0.930	0.769
The use of mobile banking has become a habit to me	0.905			
I am addicted to using mobile banking	0.852			
I must use mobile banking	0.861			
Using mobile banking has become natural to me	0.889			
BEHAVIORAL INTENTION		0.743	0.859	0.670
I intend to continue using mobile banking in the future	0.826			
I will always try to use mobile banking every time I do my banking	0.814			
I plan to use mobile banking more times	0.815			

Source: Author generated output

4.4 Divergent Validity

In assessing the independence of each construct to avoid the potential of multicollinearity bias in the regression estimates, the divergent validity of is examined by comparing the inter-construct correlation coefficients with the square root of the average variance explained (AVE). The results for both internet and mobile banking are presented in Table 4.6, with the square root of the AVEs presented in italics while the inter-construct correlation coefficients have been highlighted (Sea blue for internet banking and green for mobile banking). The results indicate that the square root of the AVE's are greater than all the estimated correlation inter-construct coefficient and demonstrates discriminant validity.

Table 4.6: Discriminant Validity results

	BI	PE	EE	SI	FC	HM	PV	HT
Internet Banking Sample								
BI	*0.899*							
PE	0.361	*0.740*						
EE	0.450	0.621	*0.874*					
SI	0.244	0.358	0.475	*0.849*				
FC	0.522	0.622	0.791	0.516	*0.849*			
HM	0.318	0.235	0.555	0.210	0.496	*0.908*		
PV	0.340	0.389	0.444	0.090	0.369	0.451	*0.857*	
HT	0.530	0.316	0.454	0.301	0.470	0.399	0.325	*0.875*
Mobile Banking Sample								
BI	*0.819*							
PE	0.286	*0.730*						
EE	0.384	0.538	*0.833*					
SI	0.224	0.235	0.456	*0.811*				
FC	0.322	0.513	0.706	0.519	*0.864*			
HM	0.244	0.368	0.607	0.333	0.609	*0.907*		
PV	0.369	0.436	0.488	0.252	0.497	0.518	*0.868*	
HT	0.446	0.290	0.441	0.343	0.404	0.472	0.458	*0.877*

Notes: BI=Behavioural intention; PE=Performance expectancy; EE=Effort expectancy; SI=Social influence; FC=Facilitating condition; HM=Hedonic motivation; PV=Perceived value; HT=Habit Source: Author generated output

4.5 Regression results: Determinants of Behavioural Intention

The result of the regression estimates on the determinants of behavioural intention to use internet banking and mobile banking are presented in Table 4.7. The model diagnostics show that the predictors explain between 41.01% of the variance of the behavioural intention to use internet banking (R^2 =0.4101) and 28.52% of the variance for behavioural intention to use mobile banking (R^2 =0.2852). Overall, the independent variables are collectively significant in explaining behavioural intention to use internet and mobile banking among SMEs in Namibia.

Table 4.7: Determinants of behavioural intention to use internet and mobile banking

Behavioural Intention:	Internet Banking		Mobile Banking	
	Coef.	*Std. Err.*	*Coef.*	*Std. Err.*
Constant	1.815***	0.590	1.630**	0.653
Performance expectancy	0.042	0.107	0.037	0.102
Effort expectancy	-0.065	0.118	0.247**	0.116
Social influence	-0.016	0.081	-0.004	0.104
Facilitating condition	0.350***	0.115	0.054	0.135
Hedonic motivation	-0.022	0.088	-0.149	0.097
Perceived value	0.115	0.092	0.181*	0.093
Habit	0.355***	0.090	0.324***	0.101
Age	-0.051	0.093	-0.041	0.113
Gender	-0.192	0.194	0.012	0.231
Qualification	-0.062	0.123	-0.207	0.147
Experience	-0.125	0.083	0.021	0.103
$F(11, 120)$	7.58		4.35	
Prob > F	0.000		0.000	
R-squared	0.4101		0.2852	
Adj R-squared	0.356		0.2196	
Hettest χ^2	2.23		0.77	
Prob>χ^2	0.1351		0.3791	
Root MSE	0.92941		1.0778	
Observations	132		132	

Note: ***, ** and * denotes significance at 1%, 5% and 10% respectively. Standard errors in parentheses;
Source: Author's generated output

From Table 4.7, the results indicate that habit has a considerable prediction power in explaining the behavioural intention to use internet and mobile banking among SMEs in Namibia (b = 0.355 at 1% for internet banking and b = 0.324 at 1% for mobile banking). The positive coefficients indicate that habit increases the behavioural intention to adopt internet and mobile banking technology among Namibian SMEs. The same conclusion is similarly evidenced by the study carried out by Moorthy et al, (2017) who argued that habit is one of the main barriers to consumer's' new technology adoption. Alalwan et al., (2015), Chemingui and Hajer, (2013); Antón et al., (2013), (Venkatesh et al., (2016), Zhang et al., (2017) and (Hanafizadeh et al., 2013) provides similar evidence on this finding.

The coefficient of facilitating condition is also observed to positively related to behavioural intention to adopt internet and mobile banking, but only statistically significant for internet at 1%. This indicates that facilitating condition only improves SMEs intention to use internet banking. This finding re-enforce the similar evidence by Tai and Ku, (2013), Chiao-Chen, (2013) and Tau and Lau. (2016).

The next significant determinants of intention to use electronic banking is effort expectancy, which is positively related to mobile banking at 5%. Consistent with Farah et al. (2018), this result indicates that consumers are always looking for technologies that simplify their activities while requiring little effort on their behalf.

Finally, the coefficient of perceived value was observed to be positive and significant at 10%, which indicates Namibian SMEs who have higher perceived value for the benefits of mobile banking services exhibit higher behavioral intentions towards mobile banking. This finding re-enforces similar evidence by Shambare (2013), Alalwan et al. (2016), Makanyeza (2017) and Farah et al. (2018).

All other control variables plays no role in the determination of the behavioural intention to adopt internet banking while experience determines the importance of mobile banking adoption.

4.5.1 Determinants of user behaviour for internet and mobile banking

The result of the logistic regression estimation to examine the likelihood of an SME using internet banking and mobile banking are presented Table 4.8. The results show that the predictors are able to explain between 44.28% and 17.37% of the variance in usage of internet banking (R^2=0.4428) and mobile banking (R^2=0.1737) respectively among SMEs in Namibia. The other test statistics (likelihood ratio, score, wald) are used to test the whether all independent variables combined significantly contributes to the outcome of the dependent variables. These tests follow the chi-square distribution (Hosmer and Lemeshow, 1989) which has P-values is greater than 0.05 which indicates the fitness of the logistic models.

Table 4.8: User behaviour for internet and mobile banking: Logistic Regression

User Behaviour	Internet Banking		Mobile Banking	
	Odds Ratio	Std. Err.	Odds Ratio	P>z
Constant	0.005***	0.009	0.094*	0.092
Performance expectancy	2.223**	0.724	1.300	0.25
Effort expectancy	1.052	0.441	0.732	0.283
Social influence	0.685	0.203	1.127	0.558
Facilitating condition	2.757**	1.171	0.811	0.376
Hedonic motivation	0.914	0.253	1.008	0.97
Perceived value	1.352	0.397	1.216	0.342
Habit	1.348	0.353	1.721***	0.007
Age	0.496**	0.152	1.335	0.156
Gender	0.779	0.452	0.799	0.609
Qualification	1.278	0.532	0.813	0.487
Experience	1.498	0.424	1.067	0.736
LR χ^2 (11)	75.57		30.11	
Prob > χ^2	0.000		0.0015	
Pseudo R2	0.4428		0.1737	
Pearson χ^2	133.61		130.12	
Prob > χ^2	0.1544		0.2289	
Log likelihood	-47.554759		-75.285656	
Observations	132		132	

Note: ***, ** and * denotes significance at 1%, 5% and 10% respectively. Standard errors in parentheses;
Source: Author's generated output

From Table 4.8, we observe facilitating condition and performance expectancy increase the likelihood of SME usage of internet banking by 2.825 times and 2.687 times respectively at 5% level of significance. Similarly, hedonic motivation is 1.486 times to highly impact the adoption of mobile banking at a significance level of 0.05 also determined by the age factor. The remaining variables are statistically insignificant (Hosmer and Lemeshow, 1898).

Finally, the effect of behavioural intention on user behaviour of electronic (internet and mobile) banking among Namibian SMEs. The model is estimated using logistic technique which examines the likelihood of behavioural intention to influence a SMEs decision to use internet and mobile banking services. From the results Table 4.9, we observe positive and significant coefficients for behavioural intention to use of internet (BI_Internet) and mobile (BI_Mobile) banking services. This indicates that intention to use electronic banking results in actual usage of electronic banking products and services. Similar findings are reported by Makanyeza (2017) in Zimbabwe.

Table 4.9: User Behaviour and behavioural intention

User Behaviour	Internet Banking		Mobile Banking	
	Odds Ratio	*Std. Err.*	*Odds Ratio*	*Std. Err.*
Constant	0.086***	0.059	0.211***	0.121
BI_Internet	2.328***	0.432		
BI_Mobile			1.632***	0.255
LR χ^2 (10)	24.97		10.71	
Prob $> \chi^2$	0.0000		0.0011	
Pseudo χ^2	0.1463		0.0588	
Pearson χ^2	2.15		2.68	
Prob $> \chi^2$	0.5425		0.4432	
Log likelihood	-72.85562		-85.76282	
Observations	132		132	

Note: BI_Internet=behavioural Intention to use internet banking; BI_Mobile=behavioural Intention to use Mobile banking ***, ** and * denotes significance at 1%, 5% and 10% respectively. Standard errors in parentheses; Source: Author's generated output

Upon examining the model used, it focused on the facilitating condition and habit as the strongest drivers of the acceptance of technology in the consumer settings (Venketash et al. 2003). This research further found that social influence and hedonic motivation has high impact on the adoption of internet banking technology in addition to the habit moderated by age and experience as well as performance expectancy moderated by experience while the use of mobile banking technology in Namibia is impacted by habit, hedonic motivation, price value and social influence.

Chapter 5

DISCUSSION, RECOMENDATIONS AND CONCLUSION

5.1   Introduction

The chapter will discuss the results from the data analysed in the chapter 4. The paper seeks to translate the findings into practical evidence, examine and compare previous research with the present study. The significance of the findings will be explained and conclusions will be drawn and linked to the studied population. All other factors contributing to challenges and implications of the study findings will be explained.

5.2   Discussion

The banking sector in Namibia has been revolutionised in the recent years after introduction of the technological banking to exploit the associated benefits and bring over the marginalised section of the population especially the small, medium enterprises into the financial stream economy. This study used UTAUT2 to better predict the actual usage of mobile and internet banking by SMEs in Namibia and advises the benefits associated with the adoptions of the electronic banking. The data was collected by using structured questionnaire to the small and medium business operators in Outapi, Oshakati and Otjiwarongo, by using UTUAT2 adopted questionnaires (Viswanath et al, 2003).

The researcher distributed 200 questionnaires to the small and medium business operator and has equally received 200 questionnaires from the SMEs. 132 have been completed and has been run using binary logistic regression model and all factors such as performance expectancy, effort expectancy, social influence, facilitating condition, hedonic motivation, price value and habit were tested for prediction of internet and mobile banking usage. The results from the tested factors were obtained of which some were found to be significant while for some factors were insignificance to the prediction of technology adoption.

- Starting first with performance and effort expectancy, the impact on the usage of internet banking technology has been tested and found to have low impact on technology use. Thus hypothesis 1 is tested in the study and rejected however effort expectancy is a positive predictor on mobile banking. According to Park et al. (2007), Small and medium business operator will always be on the look for the banking technologies that will simplify their business activities while requiring little efforts to use it. The results are as expected, thus the hypothesis 2 on mobile banking is supported.

- Social influence affect negatively the user's behaviours on behavioral intention for internet banking and has low impact on the users' behavior on uses of mobile banking technology, thus hypothesis 3 is not supported and rejected on both internet and mobile banking. Research has revealed that an SME is likely to adopt internet and mobile banking if the important others in their circles are using the same technology (Mbrokoh, 2016).

- Facilitating condition has been found to be a strong predictor and significant on the users' behavioral intention to adopt the usage of internet banking technology, thus hypothesis 4 is supported on internet banking. Venkatesh et all, (2003) rationalised his argument on this factor by saying if performance and effort expectancy are present then facilitation condition impacts on the users will be low. Alternatively facilitating condition is insignificant on users' behavioural intention on the mobile banking technology usage hence hypothesis 4 is not supported for mobile banking.

- Hedonic motivation has been tested and found to have negative impact on behavioural intention to use the internet banking thus hypothesis 5 is rejected and cannot be considered for internet and mobile banking.

- Perceived value is significant and positive determinant on behavioural intention for users' behaviour on the usage of internet banking therefore hypothesis 6 is tested and not rejected for behavioural intention because it is significant however it is considered for the uses of technology because of its significance. Similarly perceived value was tested for behavioral intention on users' behaviour for mobile banking and the result was not considered, thus hypothesis 6 is rejected for mobile banking technology adoption. According to Dootson et al, (2006) if an SME feels that the service offers advantage to the business in terms of value and performance than that SME will prefer to use that services.

- The results also find out that habit has strong impact on behavioural intention and is significant determinant on users' behaviour to use internet banking services therefore hypothesis 7 is not rejected. On mobile banking the results show strong and significant impact habit has on behavioural intention and as a significant determinant on users' behaviour hence the same hypothesis on mobile banking adoption 7 is not rejected.

5.3   Answer to Research questions and Recommendations

5.3.1 Questions

- What factors influences SMEs intention to adopt the internet and mobile banking in Namibia?

This study has demonstrated that using UTAUT2 offers accurate prediction on the SME intention to use electronic banking (internet and mobile). Other research have used different models such as Technology Acceptance Model (TAM) Technology Acceptance Models/theories which are theory of reasoned action, TAM/TAM2, motivation model, theory of planned behavior, combined TAM and TPB, model of PC utilization, innovation diffusion theory and social cognitive theory to assess factors that drive the adoption of e – banking. This study has revealed that habit has a major prediction impact on both internet and mobile banking adoption, informing that the SME are becoming proficient in the usage of the service when they use the service repeatedly. Facilitating conditions also plays a vital role in adoption of the technological banking services when the conducive conditions are set in place such as the network, availability of cellular handset and PC gadgets. The study also further showed that effort expectancy have invariably contribution to the adoption of internet and mobile banking of which that most SMEs feels that they have knowledge and resources to use and acquire the needed assets.

- What factors determines SMEs usage of internet and mobile banking?

The study further showed that the usage of internet banking is strongly influenced by performance expectancy and facilitating conditions whereby the SMEs feel that they have resources to use internet services from the localities and the service is useful to the business and provide comparative advantage by enhancing the business performance. The small and medium enterprises also believe that internet banking provide outcome expectation of their business because it provide external motivation to suppliers and customer alike. The results also shows that habit is a strong predictor for the usage of mobile banking technology of which the SMEs feel that by using the service repeatedly they were able to internalise the service and make it the ordinal way of banking then the traditional banking.

- Does SMEs intention to adopt the internet and mobile banking lead to usage of internet and mobile banking?

The study has shown the intention to adopt internet and mobile banking was explained under habit, performance and effort expectancy, social influence and facilitating condition. Other factors such as perceived value and hedonic motivation plays an insignificant role in the intention to adopt both internet and mobile banking. The research further reveals that many SMEs are intending to switch to the new banking technologies in Namibia however they are not fully motivated to use it. After conducting this study, the researcher is aiming at providing recommendation to the commercial banks, mobile and network service provider and the regulator to enhance, and increase the adoption of the new banking technologies by the SMEs in the future.

5.4   Limitation and Future Research

- This study has several limitations. The study has employed convenience sample due to the budget and time limit and has only targeted three least and semi developed towns of Outapi, Oshakati and Otjiwarongo and the results generalise the SME population across the country.

- Moreover, this study was carried at pre-adoption stage thus similar study can be conducted at different stage of consumer journey. Factors identified, including habit, performance, and effort expectancy, facilitating condition and social influence at pre-adoption stage of internet and mobile banking maybe examined at a different stage of consumer – service relationship (e.g. growth stage) to examine the users' behavioural intention and usage behaviour to use the internet and mobile banking at varying points in time.